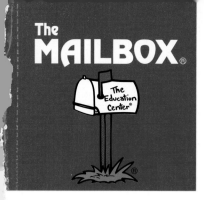

The MAILBOX®

The Education Center®

Language Arts ENVELOPE Centers

15 READY-TO-USE CENTERS

- **Capitalization**
- **Simple and Compound Sentences**
- **Verb Tenses**
- **Subject-Verb Agreement**
- **Irregular Verbs**
- **Adjectives and Adverbs**
- **Prepositions and Prepositional Phrases**

- **Punctuation**
- **Homophones**
- **Synonyms and Antonyms**
- **Fact and Opinion**
- **Prefixes and Suffixes**

Build Basic Language Arts Skills!

Managing Editor: Amy Payne

Editorial Team: Becky S. Andrews, Kimberley Bruck, Karen P. Shelton, Diane Badden, Thad H. McLaurin, Sharon Murphy, Marsha Erskine, Karen A. Brudnak, Hope Rodgers, Dorothy C. McKinney, Christine Thuman

Production Team: Lori Z. Henry, Pam Crane, Rebecca Saunders, Jennifer Tipton Cappoen, Chris Curry, Sarah Foreman, Theresa Lewis Goode, Clint Moore, Greg D. Rieves, Barry Slate, Donna K. Teal, Zane Williard, Tazmen Carlisle, Marsha Heim, Lynette Dickerson, Mark Rainey

www.themailbox.com

Another Fine Product From the Learning Centers Club®

Table of Contents

15 Envelope Centers

Skills

©2006 The Mailbox®
All rights reserved.
ISBN10 #1-56234-711-X • ISBN13 #978-156234-711-6

Manufactured in the United States
10 9 8 7 6 5 4 3 2 1

How to Use

1. Read the teacher page for each envelope center and prepare the center as directed.

2. Use the center as independent practice or for early finishers. If desired, send a center home with a student for additional practice.

3. Use the checklist on page 4 to help keep track of each student's progress.

Teacher Directions

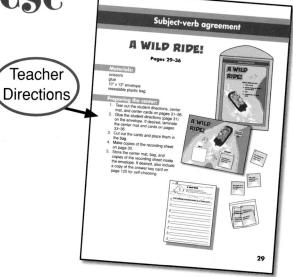

Envelope Center

Targeted Language Arts Skill

Student Directions

Center Mat

Center Cards

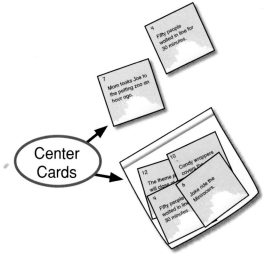

Recording Sheet

Envelope Center Checklist

Student	Are We There Yet? Capitalization	Meet Me at the Mall: Simple and compound sentences	Time Traveling: Verb tenses	A Wild Ride! Subject-verb agreement	Kick It Up! Irregular verbs	Safe and Secure? Adjectives and adverbs	Skate Time! Prepositions and phrases	Spaced Out: Commas	Alien Invasion: Quotation marks	"Hare" Spray: Homophones	Salty Synonyms: Synonyms	Movie Night: Antonyms	Band Contest: Fact and opinion	Summer Camp: Prefixes	Hanging On: Suffixes

4

Are We There Yet?

Pages 5–12

Materials:

scissors
glue
10" x 13" envelope
resealable plastic bag

Preparing the center:

1. Tear out the student directions, center mat, and center cards on pages 7–12.
2. Glue the student directions (page 7) on the envelope. If desired, laminate the center mat and cards on pages 9–12.
3. Cut out the cards and place them in the bag.
4. Make copies of the recording sheet on page 6.
5. Store the center mat, bag, and copies of the recording sheet inside the envelope. If desired, also include a copy of the answer key card on page 125 for self-checking.

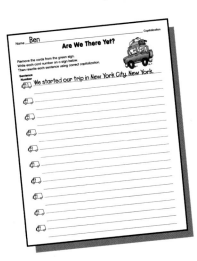

Are We There Yet?

Remove the cards from the green sign.
Then rewrite each sentence using correct capitalization.

**Sentence
Number**

_____

_____

_____

_____

_____

_____

_____

_____

_____

_____

_____

_____

_____

_____

_____

_____

Note to the teacher: Use with the directions on page 5.

Are We There Yet?

Here's what you do:

1. Sort each card on a sign.

2. Complete the recording sheet.

Are We There Yet?

Needs Capitalization

Doesn't Need Capitalization

Are We There Yet?

1. We started our trip in new york city, new york.

2. Mom said, "Don't forget the map!"

3. dad and mom took turns driving.

4. Dad used *Wild bill's road atlas* to plan the trip.

5. The view from Grandfather Mountain was lovely.

6. We drove for days and days.

7. How many Cows are in the United states?

8. I read *ann of green gables* while we traveled.

9. Spot stuck his nose out the window.

10. "let's not eat at Sammy's Slop Shop!" i exclaimed.

11. My brother kept asking, "When are we going to get there?"

12. We crossed a big river near memphis, tennessee.

13. We stopped in St. Louis for awhile.

14. We visited our cousin daniel in dallas, texas.

15. My sister loved seeing the Hoover Dam.

16. Mom got lost on elm street.

17. At last, Dad stopped and asked for directions.

18. We were supposed to turn right on Elm Street instead of left.

19. Next year, we'll go to the beach.

20. i can't wait until we get there!

Are We There Yet?
TEC61033

Are We There Yet?
TEC61033

Are We There Yet?
TEC61033

Are We There Yet?
TEC61033

Are We There Yet?
TEC61033

Are We There Yet?
TEC61033

Are We There Yet?
TEC61033

Are We There Yet?
TEC61033

Are We There Yet?
TEC61033

Are We There Yet?
TEC61033

Are We There Yet?
TEC61033

Are We There Yet?
TEC61033

Are We There Yet?
TEC61033

Are We There Yet?
TEC61033

Are We There Yet?
TEC61033

Are We There Yet?
TEC61033

Are We There Yet?
TEC61033

Are We There Yet?
TEC61033

Are We There Yet?
TEC61033

Are We There Yet?
TEC61033

Meet Me at the Mall

Pages 13–20

Materials:

scissors
glue
10" x 13" envelope
2 resealable plastic bags

Preparing the center:

1. Tear out the student directions, center mat, and center cards on pages 15–20.
2. Glue the student directions (page 15) on the envelope. If desired, laminate the center mat and cards on pages 17–20.
3. Cut out the cards and place each set in a bag.
4. Make copies of the recording sheet on page 14.
5. Store the center mat, bags, and copies of the recording sheet inside the envelope. If desired, also include a copy of the answer key card on page 125 for self-checking.

14

Meet Me at the Mall

Write on the bag the card number for each simple sentence.
Rewrite each compound sentence on the lines.
Circle the conjunctions in the compound sentences.

Compound Sentences

_____

_____

_____

_____

_____

_____

_____

Sentence Numbers

◯ ◯ ◯ ◯ ◯

Simple Sentences

Note to the teacher: Use with the directions on page 13.

Meet Me at the Mall

Here's what you do:

1. Choose a bag of cards.

2. Sort each card on a shopping bag.

3. Complete the recording sheet.

Meet Me at the Mall

Compound Sentence

Simple Sentence

Meet Me at the Mall

Use with the directions on page 13.

1. Jill and Jared love the mall.

1. Ice cream costs five dollars.

2. After school, she met a friend.

2. Jared ate a cone, but Jill saved her money.

3. Jared bought shoes, and Jill bought a necklace.

3. Pennies and nickels filled the water fountain.

4. The kids went into the bookstore, and they read the magazines.

4. Jared did not like the water, but he added a dime anyway.

5. Vendors lined the halls.

5. They watched the shoppers while sitting on the bench.

6. The two friends watched a concert on the stage.

6. Parents pushed baby strollers, and couples sat on the benches.

7. Dancers and singers entertained everyone.

7. A vendor sold hermit crabs and goldfish.

8. A man performed magic tricks, and he amazed the crowd.

8. The woman and man bought one.

9. The music rocked the stage, and people clapped their hands.

9. A policeman watched the halls, and the janitor wiped the benches.

10. Many people saw the show, and they loved it.

10. Jill's mom came to pick her up, so the two friends said goodbye.

Meet Me at the Mall
TEC61033

Meet Me at the Mall
TEC61033

Meet Me at the Mall
TEC61033

Meet Me at the Mall
TEC61033

Meet Me at the Mall
TEC61033

Meet Me at the Mall
TEC61033

Meet Me at the Mall
TEC61033

Meet Me at the Mall
TEC61033

Meet Me at the Mall
TEC61033

Meet Me at the Mall
TEC61033

Meet Me at the Mall
TEC61033

Meet Me at the Mall
TEC61033

Meet Me at the Mall
TEC61033

Meet Me at the Mall
TEC61033

Meet Me at the Mall
TEC61033

Meet Me at the Mall
TEC61033

Meet Me at the Mall
TEC61033

Meet Me at the Mall
TEC61033

Meet Me at the Mall
TEC61033

Meet Me at the Mall
TEC61033

Time Traveling

Pages 21–28

Materials:

scissors
glue
10" x 13" envelope
resealable plastic bag

Preparing the center:

1. Tear out the student directions, center mat, and center cards on pages 23–28.
2. Glue the student directions (page 23) on the envelope. If desired, laminate the center mat and cards on pages 25–28.
3. Cut out the cards and place them in the bag.
4. Make copies of the recording sheet on page 22.
5. Store the center mat, bag, and copies of the recording sheet inside the envelope. If desired, also include a copy of the answer key card on page 125 for self-checking.

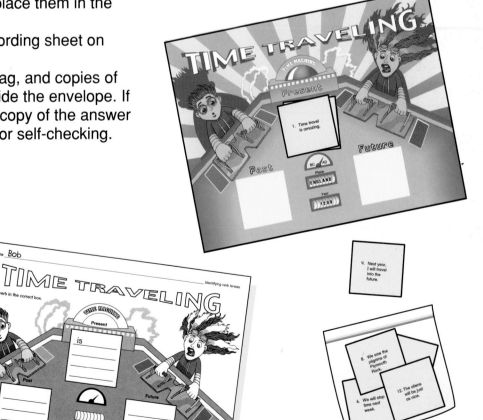

TIME TRAVELING

Name _____

22

Write each verb in the correct box.

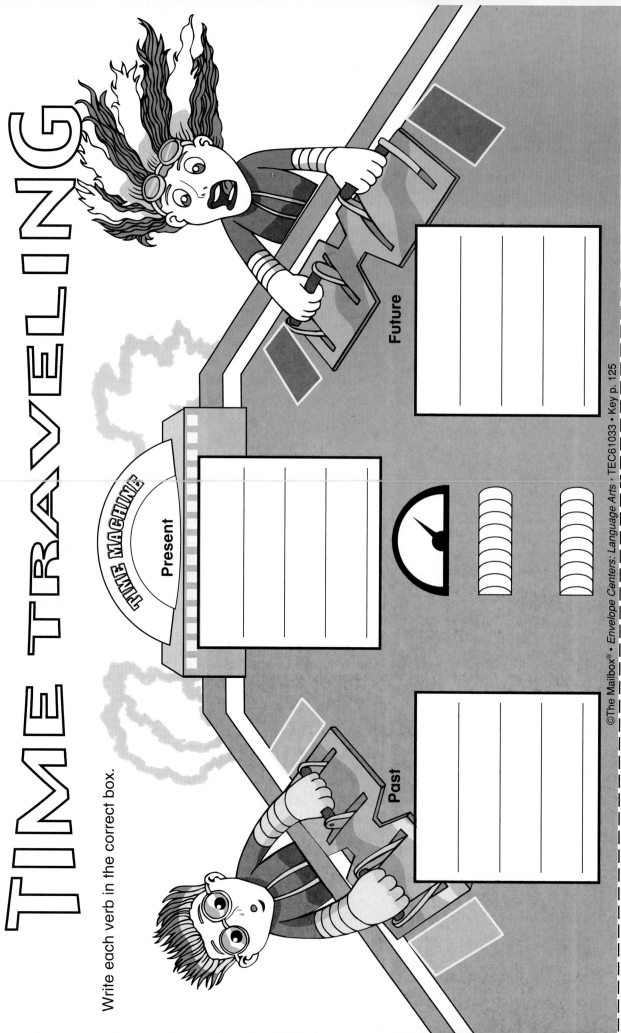

Future

Present

Past

TIME MACHINE

Note to the teacher: Use with the directions on page 21.

TIME TRAVELING

Here's what you do:

1. Sort the cards by verb tense.

2. Complete the recording sheet.

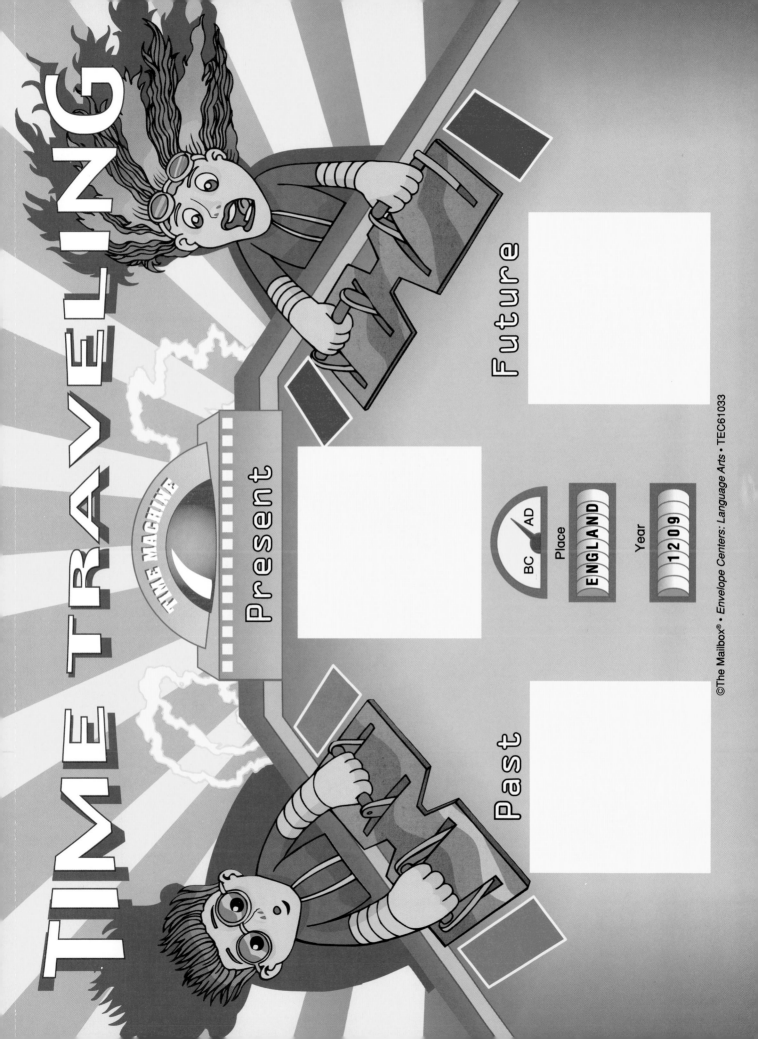

Time Traveling

1. Time travel <u>is</u> amazing.

2. One man <u>wrote</u> a book called *The Time Machine*.

3. Many still <u>dream</u> about the past.

4. Next year, I <u>will travel</u> into the future.

5. Someday, we <u>may learn</u> new facts about time.

6. We <u>will stop</u> time next week.

7. James <u>traveled</u> back to ancient Rome.

8. We <u>saw</u> the pilgrims at Plymouth Rock.

9. Some people <u>want</u> to turn back the clock.

10. Time <u>heals</u> all wounds.

11. The cavemen <u>were</u> very friendly toward us.

12. The aliens <u>will be</u> just as nice.

Time Traveling
TEC61033

Time Traveling
TEC61033

Time Traveling
TEC61033

Time Traveling
TEC61033

Time Traveling
TEC61033

Time Traveling
TEC61033

Time Traveling
TEC61033

Time Traveling
TEC61033

Time Traveling
TEC61033

Time Traveling
TEC61033

Time Traveling
TEC61033

Time Traveling
TEC61033

Subject-verb agreement

A WILD RIDE!

Pages 29–36

Materials:

scissors
glue
10" x 13" envelope
resealable plastic bag

Preparing the center:

1. Tear out the student directions, center mat, and center cards on pages 31–36.
2. Glue the student directions (page 31) on the envelope. If desired, laminate the center mat and cards on pages 33–36.
3. Cut out the cards and place them in the bag.
4. Make copies of the recording sheet on page 30.
5. Store the center mat, bag, and copies of the recording sheet inside the envelope. If desired, also include a copy of the answer key card on page 125 for self-checking.

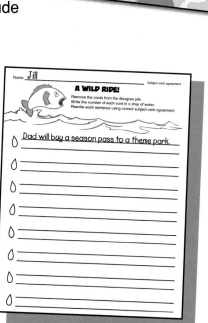

A WILD RIDE!

Remove the cards from the disagree pile.
Write the number of each card in a drop of water.
Rewrite each sentence using correct subject-verb agreement.

Note to the teacher: Use with the directions on page 29.

A WILD RIDE!

Here's what you do:

1. Take a card.

2. Decide whether the subject and verb agree.

3. Sort.

4. Complete the recording sheet.

A WILD RIDE!

WILD RIDE WATERSLIDE

Disagree

Agree

1	2	3
Dad will buys a season pass to a theme park.	Kay and I meets our friends.	My sister just ate three bags of cotton candy.

4	5	6
Fifty people waited in line for 30 minutes.	Andrew and Jake slips down the waterslide.	Jake ride the Miniracers.

7	8	9
Mom tooks Joe to the petting zoo an hour ago.	Kay and Andrew ates a snack.	Parents and kids rides the Monster Machine.

10	11	12
Candy wrappers covers the ground now.	Thomas just made two friends.	The theme park will close at nine o'clock.

A Wild Ride!
TEC61033

A Wild Ride!
TEC61033

A Wild Ride!
TEC61033

A Wild Ride!
TEC61033

A Wild Ride!
TEC61033

A Wild Ride!
TEC61033

A Wild Ride!
TEC61033

A Wild Ride!
TEC61033

A Wild Ride!
TEC61033

A Wild Ride!
TEC61033

A Wild Ride!
TEC61033

A Wild Ride!
TEC61033

KICK IT UP!

Pages 37–44

Materials:

scissors
glue
10" x 13" envelope
resealable plastic bag

Preparing the center:

1. Tear out the student directions, center mat, and center cards on pages 39–44.
2. Glue the student directions (page 39) on the envelope. If desired, laminate the center mat and cards on pages 41–44.
3. Cut out the cards and place them in the bag.
4. Make copies of the reproducible recording sheet on page 38.
5. Store the center mat, bag, and copies of the recording sheet inside the envelope. If desired, also include a copy of the answer key card on page 126 for self-checking.

KICK IT UP!

Write each verb correctly in its matching ball.

1. _____

2. _____

3. _____

4. _____

5. _____

6. _____

7. _____

8. _____

9. _____

10. _____

11. _____

12. _____

Note to the teacher: Use with the directions on page 37.

KICK IT UP!

Here's what you do:

1. Put a card on the goal.

2. Write the underlined verb correctly on the recording sheet.

3. Repeat.

KICK IT UP!

Kick It Up!

1 Before yesterday's game, we <u>singed</u> the national anthem.	**2** Our team has <u>wear</u> white jerseys to every game.	**3** Three players <u>falled</u> during the first half.
4 The goalie had <u>see</u> the ball coming.	**5** He <u>flied</u> down the field in a flash.	**6** The receiver almost <u>breaked</u> his arm.
7 The center <u>stealed</u> the ball from the other team.	**8** The bleachers <u>shaked</u> with the fans' excitement.	**9** The fans had <u>throwed</u> up their hands to cheer.
10 The players had <u>dranked</u> plenty of water.	**11** We <u>telled</u> the coach we would win the game.	**12** We <u>teached</u> the other team a lesson.

Kick It Up!

TEC61033

Kick It Up!

TEC61033

Kick It Up!

TEC61033

Kick It Up!

TEC61033

Kick It Up!

TEC61033

Kick It Up!

TEC61033

Kick It Up!

TEC61033

Kick It Up!

TEC61033

Kick It Up!

TEC61033

Kick It Up!

TEC61033

Kick It Up!

TEC61033

Kick It Up!

TEC61033

SAFE AND SECURE?

Pages 45–52

Materials:

scissors
glue
10" x 13" envelope
resealable plastic bag

Preparing the center:

1. Tear out the student directions, center mat, and center cards on pages 47–52.
2. Glue the student directions (page 47) on the envelope. If desired, laminate the center mat and cards on pages 49–52.
3. Cut out the center cards and place them in the bag.
4. Make copies of the recording sheet on page 46.
5. Store the center mat, bag, and copies of the recording sheet inside the envelope. If desired, also include a copy of the answer key card on page 126 for self-checking.

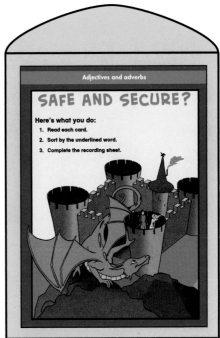

Name _____

46

SAFE AND SECURE?

Write each underlined word in the correct column.

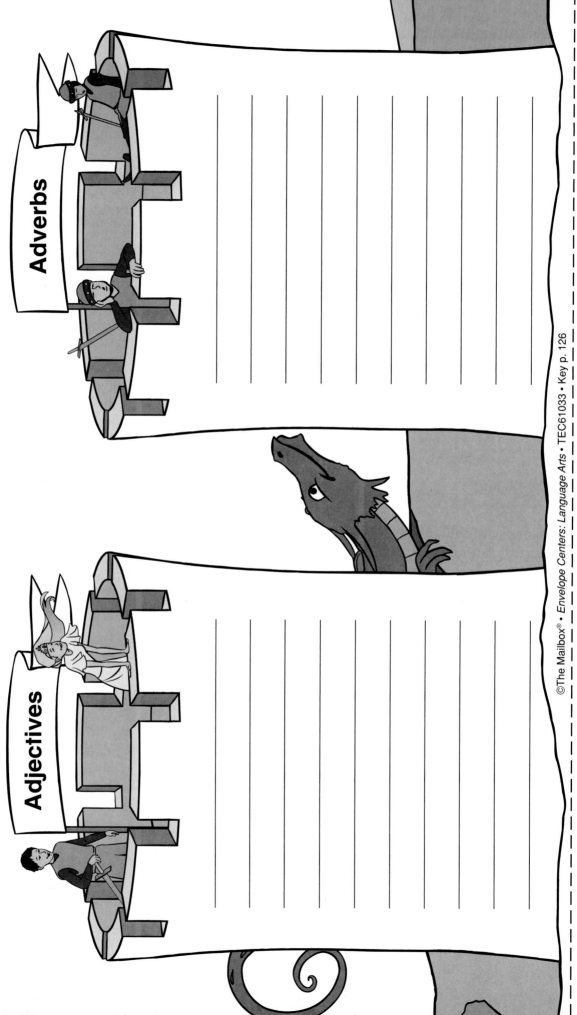

Adverbs

Adjectives

Note to the teacher: Use with the directions on page 45.

SAFE AND SECURE?

Here's what you do:

1. Read each card.

2. Sort by the underlined word.

3. Complete the recording sheet.

SAFE AND SECURE?

Adverbs

Adjectives

Safe and Secure?

1. The <u>secure</u> castle is safe from intruders.

2. Banners fly <u>boldly</u> in the wind.

3. A <u>deep</u> moat surrounds the walls.

4. Men close the drawbridge <u>nightly</u>.

5. The army patrols the <u>thick</u> walls.

6. <u>Many</u> people live inside.

7. Workers use <u>smoky</u> fires to cook.

8. <u>Crisp</u> food is grown in the gardens.

9. Grain is <u>often</u> stored in the towers.

10. Servants <u>carefully</u> record the food supplies.

11. <u>Fresh</u> water came from the well.

12. Horses are <u>safely</u> stabled.

13. The king <u>always</u> protects his lands.

14. A knight trains a <u>young</u> child.

15. A maid cleans <u>dirty</u> laundry.

16. The morning bell rings <u>loudly</u>.

17. The fire burns <u>brightly</u>.

18. Servants cook food <u>daily</u>.

19. The dragon <u>quickly</u> runs toward the castle.

20. The <u>brave</u> knight does not see the dragon.

Safe and Secure?
TEC61033

Safe and Secure?
TEC61033

Safe and Secure?
TEC61033

Safe and Secure?
TEC61033

Safe and Secure?
TEC61033

Safe and Secure?
TEC61033

Safe and Secure?
TEC61033

Safe and Secure?
TEC61033

Safe and Secure?
TEC61033

Safe and Secure?
TEC61033

Safe and Secure?
TEC61033

Safe and Secure?
TEC61033

Safe and Secure?
TEC61033

Safe and Secure?
TEC61033

Safe and Secure?
TEC61033

Safe and Secure?
TEC61033

Safe and Secure?
TEC61033

Safe and Secure?
TEC61033

Safe and Secure?
TEC61033

Safe and Secure?
TEC61033

SKATE TIME!

Pages 53–60

Materials:

scissors
glue
10" x 13" envelope

Preparing the center:

1. Tear out the student directions, center mat, and sentence strips on pages 55–60.
2. Glue the student directions (page 55) on the envelope. If desired, laminate the center mat and strips on pages 57–60.
3. Cut out the strips and cut slits in the center mat where indicated. Thread one strip through the slits.
4. Make copies of the reproducible recording sheet on page 54.
5. Store the center mat, the second sentence strip, and copies of the recording sheet inside the envelope. If desired, also include a copy of the answer key card on page 126 for self-checking.

53

Identifying prepositions and prepositional phrases

SKATE TIME!

Write each prepositional phrase on its matching skateboard.
Circle the preposition.

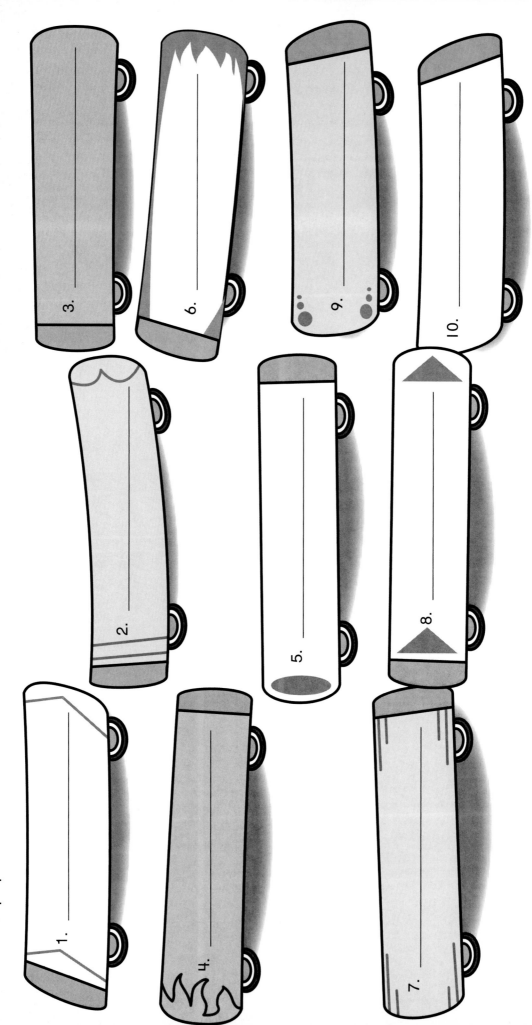

©The Mailbox® • Envelope Centers: Language Arts • TEC61033 • Key p. 126

Note to the teacher: Use with the directions on page 53.

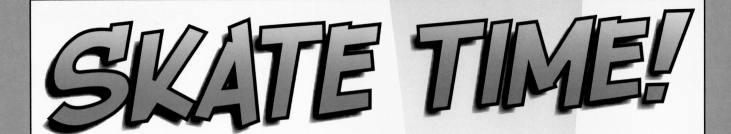

SKATE TIME!

Here's what you do:

1. Slide the strip to 1.

2. Write the prepositional phrase on the recording sheet.

3. Circle the preposition.

4. Slide the strip and repeat.

SKATE TIME!

Skate Time!

Strip A
1. She flipped her board above her head.
2. People watched from the stands.
3. He leaned into the turn.
4. She sped past the skaters.
5. Pets are not allowed inside the park.
6. We ate our snacks during the break.
7. We like to sit near the front.
8. The skateboard slipped beneath the bleachers.
9. Drake pushed his board up the ramp.
10. I'll meet you at the contest.

Strip B
1. Across the field, I spotted the skaters.
2. She kept her eyes on the path.
3. They raced around the ramp.
4. Among the skaters, he was thought to be the best.
5. He kept the board within his reach.
6. I jumped as the runaway board flew toward me.
7. I wasn't sure I could skate until now.
8. He has led throughout the day.
9. I watched two skaters speed down the sidewalk.
10. The skater went through the tunnel.

Spaced Out

Pages 61–68

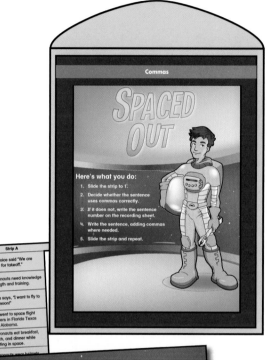

Materials:

scissors
glue
10" x 13" envelope

Preparing the center:

1. Tear out the student directions, center mat, and sentence strips on pages 63–68.

2. Glue the student directions (page 63) on the envelope. If desired, laminate the center mat and strips on pages 65–68.

3. Cut out the strips and cut slits in the center mat where indicated. Thread one strip through the slits.

4. Make copies of the recording sheet on page 62.

5. Store the center mat, the second sentence strip, and copies of the recording sheet inside the envelope. If desired, also include a copy of the answer key card on page 126 for self-checking.

Name

Spaced Out

Sentence Number

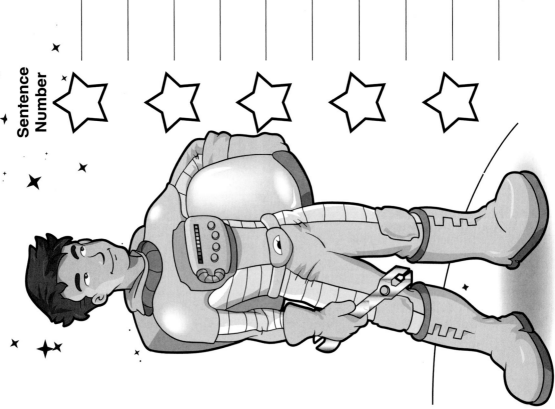

Note to the teacher: Use with the directions on page 61.

SPACED OUT

Here's what you do:

1. Slide the strip to 1.

2. Decide whether the sentence uses commas correctly.

3. If it does not, write the sentence number on the recording sheet.

4. Write the sentence, adding commas where needed.

5. Slide the strip and repeat.

SPACED OUT

Spaced Out

Strip A

10. The voice said "We are ready for takeoff."

9. Astronauts need knowledge strength and training.

8. Anna says, "I want to fly to the moon!"

7. We went to space flight centers in Florida Texas and Alabama.

6. Astronauts eat breakfast, lunch, and dinner while floating in space.

5. Astronauts wear helmets gloves and suits.

4. The three astronauts yelled, "Let's go!"

3. "Wow! Look at that!" exclaimed the captain.

2. He announced "The shuttle will launch at three o'clock today."

1. The earth, the moon, and the sun float in space.

Strip B

10. Space jobs include research repair and construction.

9. Jim Sue and Randy watched the shuttle take off.

8. Megan yelled "I see a shooting star!"

7. You can see land, clouds, and water when you're in space.

6. "The satellite will be launched and set up" said the tour guide.

5. Rita asked, "What is it like to be upside down in space?"

4. Jason read books searched the Internet and asked lots of questions.

3. During our tour, we saw pictures, models, and spaceships.

2. Tim asked, "Where do the astronauts sit?"

1. "Will kids ever visit other planets?" asked Lucy.

ALIEN INVASION

Pages 69–76

Materials:

scissors
glue
10" x 13" envelope

Preparing the center:

1. Tear out the student directions, center mat, and sentence strips on pages 71–76.
2. Glue the student directions (page 71) on the envelope. If desired, laminate the center mat and strips on pages 73–76.
3. Cut out the strips and cut slits in the center mat where indicated. Thread one strip through the slits.
4. Make copies of the recording sheet on page 70.
5. Store the center mat, the second sentence strip, and copies of the recording sheet inside the envelope. If desired, also include a copy of the answer key card on page 127 for self-checking.

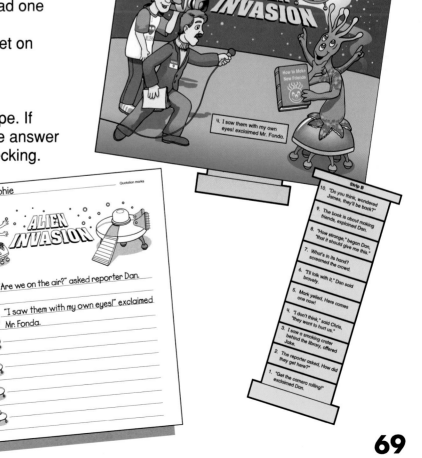

Sentence Number

 _____

_____

 _____

_____

 _____

_____

 _____

_____

 _____

_____

 _____

_____

©The Mailbox® • *Envelope Centers: Language Arts* • TEC61033 • Key p. 127

70 **Note to the teacher:** Use with the directions on page 69.

ALIEN INVASION

Here's what you do:

1. Slide the strip to 1.

2. Decide whether the sentence uses quotation marks correctly.

3. If it does not, write the sentence number on the recording sheet.

4. Write the sentence, adding quotation marks where needed.

5. Slide the strip and repeat.

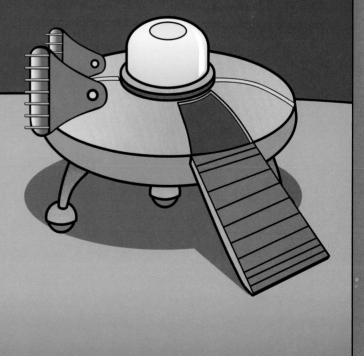

Alien Invasion

Strip A

10. "I don't believe it," mumbled the mother.

9. The little girl said, They have green hair.

8. "How many," asked Mary, do you think there are?

7. "My aunt Lou says they ate her apple pie," said a small boy.

6. One man screamed, UFO's are coming!

5. A lady asked, What do they want from us?

4. I saw them with my own eyes! exclaimed Mr. Fonda.

3. "Is it true," asked Dan, "that aliens have landed in our town?"

2. Dan began, "Good afternoon. Welcome to *News Today*."

1. "Are we on the air? asked reporter Dan.

Strip B

10. "Do you think, wondered James, they'll be back?"

9. The book is about making friends, explained Dan.

8. "How strange," began Dan, "that it should give me this."

7. What's in its hand? screamed the crowd.

6. "I'll talk with it," Dan said bravely.

5. Mark yelled, Here comes one now!

4. "I don't think," said Chris, "they want to hurt us."

3. I saw a smoking crater behind the library, offered Jake.

2. The reporter asked, How did they get here?"

1. "Get the camera rolling!" exclaimed Dan.

Alien Invasion
TEC61033

Alien Invasion
TEC61033

"HARE" SPRAY

Pages 77–84

Materials:

scissors
glue
10" x 13" envelope
resealable plastic bag

Preparing the center:

1. Tear out the student directions, center mat, and center cards on pages 79–84.
2. Glue the student directions (page 79) on the envelope. If desired, laminate the center mat and cards on pages 81–84.
3. Cut out the cards and place them in the bag.
4. Make copies of the recording sheet on page 78.
5. Store the center mat, bag, and copies of the recording sheet inside the envelope. If desired, also include a copy of the answer key card on page 127 for self-checking.

Name _____

78

"HARE" SPRAY

Remove the cards from the trash
can on the mat.
Write each card number in a box.
Then write the correct homophone
on the line.

Corrected Homphones

_____
_____
_____
_____
_____
_____
_____
_____

©The Mailbox® • *Envelope Centers: Language Arts* • TEC61033 • Key p. 127

Note to the teacher: Use with the directions on page 77.

"HARE" SPRAY

Here's what you do:

1. Decide whether each homophone is used correctly.

2. Sort.

3. Complete the recording sheet.

"Hare" Spray

1. The stylist covered my head in <u>hair</u> spray.

2. I want to <u>dye</u> my hair green for the contest.

3. She looked at my hair and said, "Your curls are <u>grate</u>!"

4. What <u>style</u> of cut would you prefer?

5. I had to <u>paws</u> and think.

6. She combed my hair into a flowing <u>Maine</u>.

7. I use <u>mousse</u> to calm down my frizzy hair.

8. This is my <u>forth</u> visit to this stylist.

9. She <u>billed</u> me for the full amount.

10. I looked through magazines to <u>chews</u> a style.

11. When I saw the results, I began to <u>bawl</u>.

12. The haircut was worth every <u>scent</u>.

13. I could smell chemicals in the <u>heir</u>.

14. My mom was <u>so</u> surprised.

15. She asked if I wanted to come again next <u>weak</u>.

"Hare" Spray
TEC61033

"Hare" Spray
TEC61033

"Hare" Spray
TEC61033

"Hare" Spray
TEC61033

"Hare" Spray
TEC61033

"Hare" Spray
TEC61033

"Hare" Spray
TEC61033

"Hare" Spray
TEC61033

"Hare" Spray
TEC61033

"Hare" Spray
TEC61033

"Hare" Spray
TEC61033

"Hare" Spray
TEC61033

"Hare" Spray
TEC61033

"Hare" Spray
TEC61033

"Hare" Spray
TEC61033

Salty Synonyms

Pages 85–92

Materials:

scissors
glue
10" x 13" envelope
resealable plastic bag

Preparing the center:

1. Tear out the student directions, center mat, and center cards on pages 87–92.
2. Glue the student directions (page 87) on the envelope. If desired, laminate the center mat and cards on pages 89–92.
3. Cut out the cards and place them in the bag.
4. Make copies of the recording sheet on page 86.
5. Store the center mat, bag, and copies of the recording sheet inside the envelope. If desired, also include a copy of the answer key card on page 127 for self-checking.

SALTY SYNONYMS

1. _____
_____

2. _____
_____

3. _____
_____

5. _____

4. _____
_____

6. _____
_____

7. _____
_____

9. _____
_____

8. _____
_____

10. _____
_____

11. _____
_____

12. _____
_____

Note to the teacher: Use with the directions on page 85.

SALTY SYNONYMS

Here's what you do:

1. Put a blue card on the pirate ship.

2. Find the matching yellow synonym card and put it on the X.

3. Write the word pair on the recording sheet.

4. Repeat.

SALTY SYNONYMS

Salty Synonyms

funny	courageous	mend	fragile
exit	forget	same	vacant
weak	thankful	silent	hurry
quiet	flimsy	identical	grateful
repair	breakable	brave	empty
overlook	rush	leave	humorous

Salty Synonyms
TEC61033

Salty Synonyms
TEC61033

Salty Synonyms
TEC61033

Salty Synonyms
TEC61033

Salty Synonyms
TEC61033

Salty Synonyms
TEC61033

Salty Synonyms
TEC61033

Salty Synonyms
TEC61033

Salty Synonyms
TEC61033

Salty Synonyms
TEC61033

Salty Synonyms
TEC61033

Salty Synonyms
TEC61033

Salty Synonyms
TEC61033

Salty Synonyms
TEC61033

Salty Synonyms
TEC61033

Salty Synonyms
TEC61033

Salty Synonyms
TEC61033

Salty Synonyms
TEC61033

Salty Synonyms
TEC61033

Salty Synonyms
TEC61033

Salty Synonyms
TEC61033

Salty Synonyms
TEC61033

Salty Synonyms
TEC61033

Salty Synonyms
TEC61033

MOVIE NIGHT

Pages 93–100

Materials:

scissors
glue
10" x 13" envelope
resealable plastic bag

Preparing the center:

1. Tear out the student directions, center mat, and center cards on pages 95–100.
2. Glue the student directions (page 95) on the envelope. If desired, laminate the center mat and cards on pages 97–100.
3. Cut out the cards and place them in the bag.
4. Make copies of the recording sheet on page 94.
5. Store the center mat, bag, and copies of the recording sheet inside the envelope. If desired, also include a copy of the answer key card on page 127 for self-checking.

Name

MOVIE NIGHT

©The Mailbox® • Envelope Centers: Language Arts • TEC61033 • Key p. 127

Note to the teacher: Use with the directions on page 93.

MOVIE NIGHT

Here's what you do:

1. Put a blue card on the television.

2. Find the matching green antonym card and put it on the remote control.

3. Write the word pair on the recording sheet.

4. Repeat.

MOVIE GUIDE

MOVIE NIGHT

Movie Night

major	bitter	brief	forbid
deep	arrive	valuable	neat
sick	plain	private	forgive
shallow	healthy	minor	public
allow	sloppy	worthless	sweet
blame	long	fancy	depart

Movie Night
TEC61033

Movie Night
TEC61033

Movie Night
TEC61033

Movie Night
TEC61033

Movie Night
TEC61033

Movie Night
TEC61033

Movie Night
TEC61033

Movie Night
TEC61033

Movie Night
TEC61033

Movie Night
TEC61033

Movie Night
TEC61033

Movie Night
TEC61033

Movie Night
TEC61033

Movie Night
TEC61033

Movie Night
TEC61033

Movie Night
TEC61033

Movie Night
TEC61033

Movie Night
TEC61033

Movie Night
TEC61033

Movie Night
TEC61033

BAND CONTEST

Pages 101–108

Materials:

scissors
glue
10" x 13" envelope
resealable plastic bag

Preparing the center:

1. Tear out the student directions, center mat, and center cards on pages 103–108.
2. Glue the student directions (page 103) on the envelope. If desired, laminate the center mat and cards on pages 105–108.
3. Cut out the cards and place them in the bag.
4. Make copies of the recording sheet on page 102.
5. Store the center mat, bag, and copies of the recording sheet inside the envelope. If desired, also include a copy of the answer key card on page 128 for self-checking.

Name _____

102

BAND CONTEST

Write each sentence number on the correct piece of equipment.

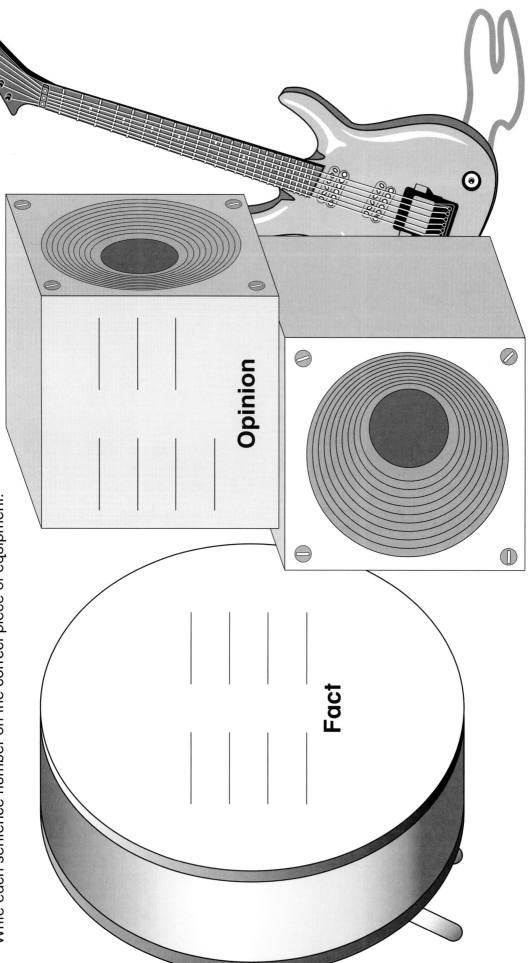

Opinion

Fact

Note to the teacher: Use with the directions on page 101.

BAND CONTEST

Here's what you do:

1. Decide whether each sentence is a fact or an opinion.

2. Sort.

3. Complete the recording sheet.

THE BOOGIE-WOOGIES

BAND CONTEST

Opinion

Fact

THE BOOGIE-WOOGIES

Band Contest

1. The Boogie-Woogies performed last Tuesday.

2. Mark Woogie is the best bass guitar player.

3. I love the sound of the drums.

4. Last year, they won first place in the Beat, Bump, and Boom Band Contest.

5. Jake Boogie broke his thumb.

6. Their music is too loud.

7. Stacey Boogie plays the drums.

8. Mark's speaker blew a fuse during his performance.

9. The lead singer, Angel, sings like an angel.

10. The Kickin' Kangoos have a smoother sound.

11. The Kangoos are not good enough to beat the Woogies.

12. The Kickin' Kangoos started their band in England.

13. This year's contest will be close.

14. Our family traveled from Texas to see the bands play.

15. Angel's hometown is in Kansas.

Band Contest
TEC61033

Band Contest
TEC61033

Band Contest
TEC61033

Band Contest
TEC61033

Band Contest
TEC61033

Band Contest
TEC61033

Band Contest
TEC61033

Band Contest
TEC61033

Band Contest
TEC61033

Band Contest
TEC61033

Band Contest
TEC61033

Band Contest
TEC61033

Band Contest
TEC61033

Band Contest
TEC61033

Band Contest
TEC61033

SUMMER CAMP

Pages 109–116

Materials:

scissors
glue
10" x 13" envelope

Preparing the center:

1. Tear out the student directions, center mat, and word strips on pages 111–116.
2. Glue the student directions (page 111) on the envelope. If desired, laminate the center mat and strips on pages 113–116.
3. Cut out the strips and cut slits on the center mat where indicated. Thread one strip through the slits.
4. Make copies of the recording sheet on page 110.
5. Store the center mat, the second word strip, and copies of the recording sheet inside the envelope. If desired, also include a copy of the answer key card on page 128 for self-checking.

SUMMER CAMP

1. _____

2. _____

3. _____

4. _____

5. _____

6. _____

7. _____

8. _____

9. _____

10. _____

Note to the teacher: Use with the directions on page 109.

SUMMER CAMP

CABIN 1

Here's what you do:

1. Slide the strip to 1.

2. Look at the prefixes on the mat.

3. Decide which prefix added to the word will make a new word.

4. Write the new word on the recording sheet.

5. Slide the strip and repeat.

SUMMER CAMP

un-

re-

dis-

Summer Camp

Strip A
1. supply
2. safe
3. agree
4. turn
5. afraid
6. believe
7. clear
8. paint
9. copy
10. known

Strip B
1. read
2. continue
3. certain
4. type
5. ready
6. funny
7. try
8. wanted
9. honest
10. measure

Summer Camp
TEC61033

Summer Camp
TEC61033

116

HANGING ON

Pages 117–124

Materials:

scissors
glue
10" x 13" envelope
resealable plastic bag

Preparing the center:

1. Tear out the student directions, center mat, and center cards on pages 119–124.
2. Glue the student directions (page 119) on the envelope. If desired, laminate the center mat and cards on pages 121–124.
3. Cut out the cards and place them in the bag.
4. Make copies of the recording sheet on page 118.
5. Store the center mat, bag, and copies of the recording sheet inside the envelope. If desired, also include a copy of the answer key card on page 128 for self-checking.

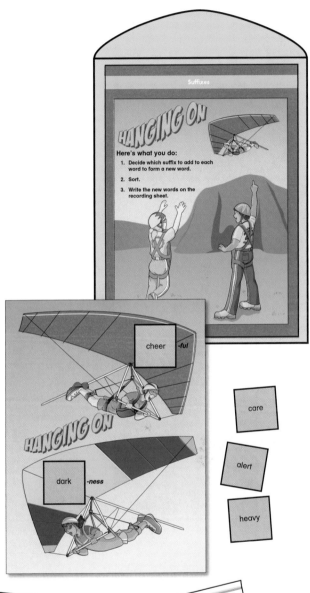
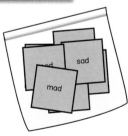

-ful	-ness
_____	_____
_____	_____
_____	_____
_____	_____
_____	_____
_____	_____
_____	_____
_____	_____

©The Mailbox® • *Envelope Centers: Language Arts* • TEC61033 • Key p. 128

118 **Note to the teacher:** Use with the directions on page 117.

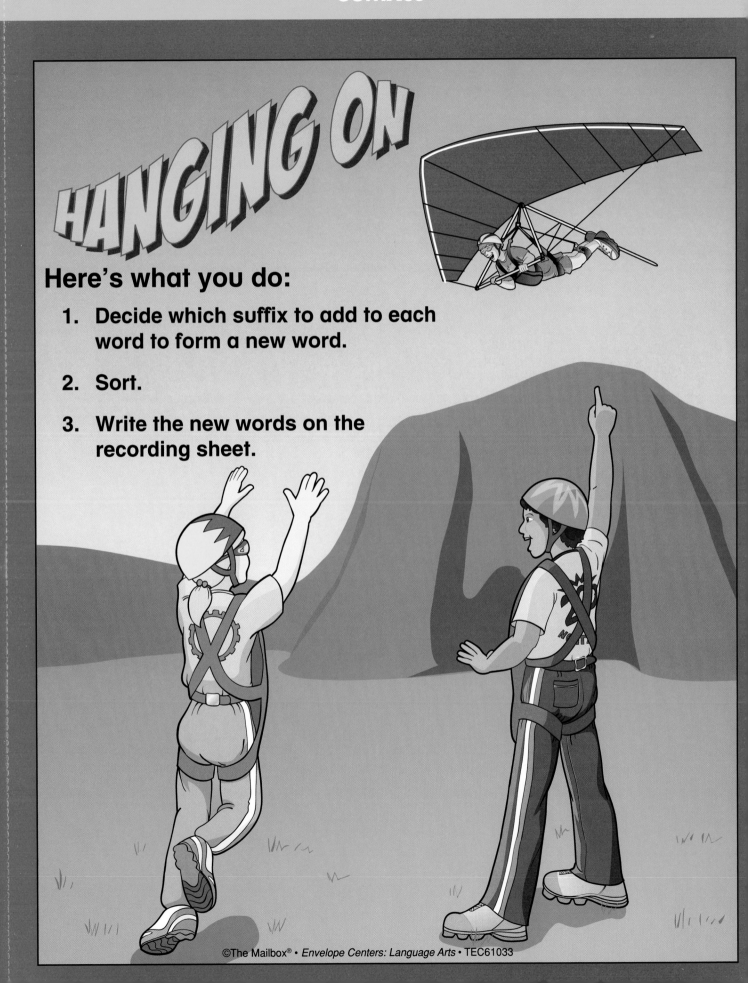

HANGING ON

Here's what you do:

1. Decide which suffix to add to each word to form a new word.

2. Sort.

3. Write the new words on the recording sheet.

-ful

HANGING ON

-ness

Hanging On

thought	cheer	care	fear
hand	hope	peace	help
polite	alert	heavy	dark
sad	good	mad	tired

Hanging On
TEC61033

Hanging On
TEC61033

Hanging On
TEC61033

Hanging On
TEC61033

Hanging On
TEC61033

Hanging On
TEC61033

Hanging On
TEC61033

Hanging On
TEC61033

Hanging On
TEC61033

Hanging On
TEC61033

Hanging On
TEC61033

Hanging On
TEC61033

Hanging On
TEC61033

Hanging On
TEC61033

Hanging On
TEC61033

Hanging On
TEC61033

Answer Keys

Page 6: "Are We There Yet?"

1. We started our trip in New York City, New York.
3. Dad and Mom took turns driving.
4. Dad used *Wild Bill's Road Atlas* to plan the trip.
7. How many cows are in the United States?
8. I read *Ann of Green Gables* while we traveled.
10. "Let's not eat at Sammy's Slop Shop!" I exclaimed.
12. We crossed a big river near Memphis, Tennessee.
14. We visited our cousin Daniel in Dallas, Texas.
16. Mom got lost on Elm Street.
20. I can't wait until we get there!

Page 14: "Meet Me at the Mall"

Purple Center Cards
Simple Sentences: 1, 2, 5, 6, 7
Compound Sentences:

3. Jared bought shoes, (and) Jill bought a necklace.
4. The kids went into the bookstore, (and) they read the magazines.
8. A man performed magic tricks, (and) he amazed the crowd.
9. The music rocked the stage, (and) people clapped their hands.
10. Many people saw the show, (and) they loved it.

Green Center Cards
Simple Sentences: 1, 3, 5, 7, 8
Compound Sentences:

2. Jared ate a cone, (but) Jill saved her money.
4. Jared did not like the water, (but) he added a dime anyway.
6. Parents pushed baby strollers, (and) couples sat on the benches.
9. A policeman watched the halls, (and) the janitor wiped the benches.
10. Jill's mom came to pick her up, (so) the two friends said goodbye.

Page 22: "Time Traveling"

Past: wrote, traveled, saw, were
Present: is, dream, want, heals
Future: will travel, may learn, will stop, will be

Page 30: "A Wild Ride!"

Correct: 3, 4, 11, 12

1. Dad will **buy** a season pass to a theme park.
2. Kay and I **meet** our friends.
5. Andrew and Jake **slip** down the waterslide.
6. Jake **rides** the Miniracers.
7. Mom **took** Joe to the petting zoo an hour ago.
8. Kay and Andrew **ate** a snack.
9. Parents and kids **ride** the Monster Machine.
10. Candy wrappers **cover** the ground now.

Page 38: "Kick It Up!"

1. sang
2. worn
3. fell
4. seen
5. flew
6. broke
7. stole
8. shook
9. thrown
10. drunk
11. told
12. taught

Page 46: "Safe and Secure?"

Adjectives: secure, deep, thick, many, smoky, crisp, fresh, young, dirty, brave

Adverbs: boldly, nightly, often, carefully, safely, always, loudly, brightly, daily, quickly

Page 54: "Skate Time"

Strip A

1. (above) her head
2. (from) the stands
3. (into) the turn
4. (past) the skaters
5. (inside) the park
6. (during) the break
7. (near) the front
8. (beneath) the bleachers
9. (up) the ramp
10. (at) the contest

Strip B

1. (Across) the field
2. (on) the path
3. (around) the ramp
4. (Among) the skaters
5. (within) his reach
6. (toward) me
7. (until) now
8. (throughout) the day
9. (down) the sidewalk
10. (through) the tunnel

Page 62: "Spaced Out"

Strip A

Correct: 1, 3, 4, 6, and 8

2. He announced, "The shuttle will launch at three o'clock today."
5. Astronauts wear helmets, gloves, and suits.
7. We went to space flight centers in Florida, Texas, and Alabama.
9. Astronauts need knowledge, strength, and training.
10. The voice said, "We are ready for takeoff."

Strip B

Correct: 1, 2, 3, 5, and 7

4. Jason read books, searched the Internet, and asked lots of questions.
6. "The satellite will be launched and set up," said the tour guide.
8. Megan yelled, "I see a shooting star!"
9. Jim, Sue, and Randy watched the shuttle take off.
10. Space jobs include research, repair, and construction.

Page 70: "Alien Invasion"

Strip A
Correct: 2, 3, 7, 10

1. "Are we on the air?" asked reporter Dan.
4. "I saw them with my own eyes!" exclaimed Mr. Fonda.
5. A lady asked, "What do they want from us?"
6. One man screamed, "UFO's are coming!"
8. "How many," asked Mary, "do you think there are?"
9. The little girl said, "They have green hair."

Strip B
Correct: 1, 4, 6, 8

2. The reporter asked, "How did they get here?"
3. "I saw a smoking crater behind the library," offered Jake.
5. Mark yelled, "Here comes one now!"
7. "What's in its hand?" screamed the crowd.
9. "The book is about making friends," explained Dan.
10. "Do you think," wondered James, "they'll be back?"

Page 78: "'Hare' Spray"

Correct: 1, 2, 4, 7, 9, 11, and 14

3. great
5. pause
6. mane
8. fourth
10. choose
12. cent
13. air
15. week

Page 86: "Salty Synonyms"

funny, humorous
courageous, brave
mend, repair
fragile, breakable
exit, leave
forget, overlook
same, identical
vacant, empty
weak, flimsy
thankful, grateful
silent, quiet
hurry, rush

Page 94: "Movie Night"

major, minor
bitter, sweet
brief, long
forbid, allow
deep, shallow
arrive, depart
valuable, worthless
neat, sloppy
sick, healthy
plain, fancy
private, public
forgive, blame

Page 102: "Band Contest"

Fact: 1, 4, 5, 7, 8, 12, 14, 15
Opinion: 2, 3, 6, 9, 10, 11, 13

Page 110: "Summer Camp"

Strip A
1. resupply
2. unsafe
3. disagree
4. return
5. unafraid
6. disbelieve
7. unclear
8. repaint
9. recopy
10. unknown

Strip B
1. reread
2. discontinue
3. uncertain
4. retype
5. unready
6. unfunny
7. retry
8. unwanted
9. dishonest
10. remeasure

Page 118: "Hanging On"

Order of answers will vary.
-ful
thoughtful
cheerful
careful
fearful
handful
hopeful
peaceful
helpful

-ness
politeness
alertness
heaviness
darkness
sadness
goodness
madness
tiredness